a year in the life of **glencoe** bill birkett

FRANCES LINCOLN

a year in the life of glencoe bill birkett

Many thanks
To my family: Sue, my wife; Rowan and William for magical days in
Glencoe. To Mary Jenner and Dave Birkett for the latest climbing beta
and all the many climbers with whom I've shared incomparable days
in the hills. To Andrew Sheehan for his company and knowledge on
the flora and fauna and for taking my excellent portrait photograph
used on the jacket. To Mark Murray for a memorable day on Aonach
Eagach. To all the local climbers whose words, images and guidance
have been inspirational – particularly Cubby Cuthbertson, Ed Grindley,
Kev Howett and Hamish MacInnes, whose guidebooks have
revolutionised climbing in Scotland. To all those at the National Trust
for Scotland Information Centre who proffered their knowledge
– particularly Paul Morgan whose understanding of the prehistoric
landscape is quite breathtaking. To Edward Daynes for his help and
hospitality, all the staff at the Clachaig Hotel, and similarly those at
the Kingshouse Hotel for their excellent hospitality and for keeping
my son amused with the biggest black dog in the world. To my mates
in the SOGs (Sad Old Gits), particularly Mark Squires and George
Sharpe who have never held back an opinion of my work! To
bravehearts John Nicoll and Kate Cave of Frances Lincoln for
publishing this book. To Jane Havell for producing a fine balance
of the material. To those protective bodies and groups who care
about Glencoe and seek to protect its unique character and beauty,
particularly the National Trust for Scotland and the Scottish
Mountaineering Club.

Bill Birkett Photo Library
Bill Birkett has an extensive photographic library covering all of
Britain's mountains and wild places including one of the most
comprehensive collections of photographs of the English Lake District.
For information or pictures, please telephone 015394 37420 or
e-mail bill.birkett1@btopenworld.com

*TITLE PAGE: A wonderful evening as the light rapidly disappears and
hues crimson to dark purple mark sundown in the west. Over the
quiet waters of Loch Linnhe the black silhouettes of the distant hills
of Ardgour are seen from North Ballachulish. So many mountains
to climb, so little time!*

Frances Lincoln Limited
4 Torriano Mews
Torriano Avenue
London NW5 2RZ

A Year in the Life of Glencoe
Copyright © 2005 Frances Lincoln Limited

Text and photographs copyright © 2005 Bill Birkett
Map on page 6 by Martin Bagness
Edited and designed by Jane Havell Associates

First Frances Lincoln edition 2005

Bill Birkett has asserted his moral right to be identified as Author of this
Work in accordance with the Copyright, Designs and Patents Act 1988

British Library cataloguing-in-publication data
A catalogue record for this book is available from
the British Library

ISBN 0-7112-2551-6

Printed in Singapore

contents

glencoe introduction

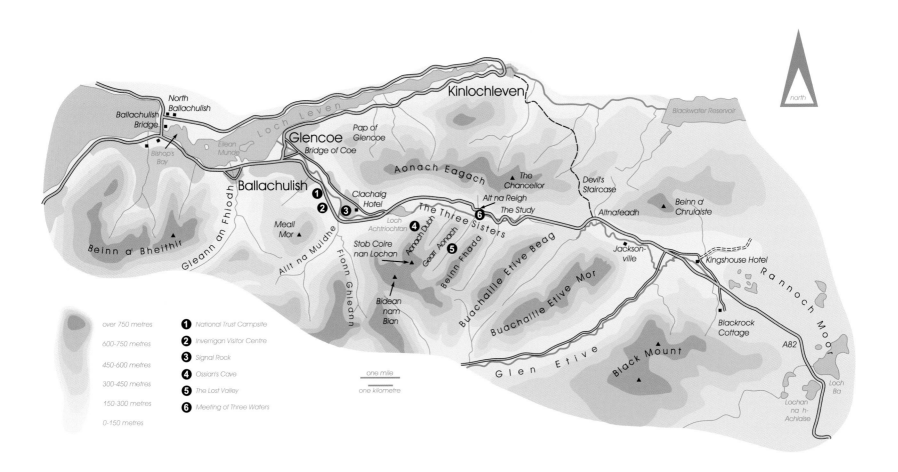

North

Kinlochleven

Blackwater Reservoir

North Ballachulish

Ballachulish Bridge

Loch Leven

Eilean Munde

Bishop's Bay

Glencoe

Bridge of Coe

Pap of Glencoe

Aonach Eagach

The Chancellor

Devil's Staircase

Ballachulish

Clachaig Hotel

Alt na Reigh

The Study

Altnafeadh

Beinn a' Chrulaiste

Gleann an Fhiodh

Meall Mor

Loch Achtriochtan

The Three Sisters

Aonach Dubh

Beinn a' Bheithir

Alt na Muidhe

Fionn Ghleann

Stob Coire nan Lochan

Gear Aonach

Beinn Fhada

Buachaille Etive Beag

Jacksonville

Kingshouse Hotel

Rannoch Moor

Bidean nam Bian

Buachaille Etive Mor

Blackrock Cottage

A82

Glen Etive

Black Mount

Loch Ba

Lochan na h-Achlaise

	over 750 metres		❶ National Trust Campsite
	600-750 metres		❷ Inverrigan Visitor Centre
	450-600 metres		❸ Signal Rock
	300-450 metres		❹ Ossian's Cave
	150-300 metres		❺ The Lost Valley
	0-150 metres		❻ Meeting of Three Waters

one mile

one kilometre

As the road north rises inexorably beyond Loch Tulla and the Bridge of Orchy, a slender rowan splits a boulder in half (page 18). At first you may wonder, how can this be? How can something so slight, so intricate and elegant flourish out of hard rock? I have travelled this way since I was a babe in arms; as a mountaineer, heartened by its symbolism, let me explain. This is no ordinary sapling. It's the magical mountain ash and talisman – a key that opens the door to the spectacular heartland of the Western Highlands of Scotland. This is the beginning of the road to Glencoe.

It is extremely fortuitous that this road first tastes the wastelands of Rannoch Moor, its myriad lochans and vast open spaces, its desolate, savage, beautiful wildness. You pass beneath the oft snow-clad Black Mount and by the remote Kingshouse Hotel nestling beneath the pyramidal blood-red rhyolite of Buachaille Etive Mor – perhaps Britain's most perfect mountain. If you didn't experience this caressing and heightening of the senses, if you were to fall directly into the depths of Britain's most famous glen, then the impact may just prove a little too much.

Enclosed by sweeping bastions of rock that stretch a thousand metres to touch the sky, the North West Highland's Glencoe plunges from the wilds of Rannoch Moor to the burial isles of Eilean Munde. Shaped by ancient volcanoes, Ice Age glaciers and the attrition of wind and rain, it is a raw landscape of awesome proportion – one of the most spectacular in Britain.

The overall first impression is of impenetrable towering heights, dark rock and huge forces that make the individual puny and inconsequential compared with the limitless forces of nature thrusting from either side. The Three Sisters, the rocky bastions of the south side, the Chancellor and the pinnacles and notches of the Aonach Eagach Ridge on the north embrace a primitive, primeval world of verticality and ruptured rock, with hanging chasms and tottering fans of scree and boulder which add to a feeling of insecurity. Even the breaks in the ramparts

offer false promise, for on closer scrutiny they lead to further formidable steeps. The Lost Valley beyond the boulder choke appears to end at the blackness of the Lost Valley Buttress. The rift between Gearr Aonach and Aonach Dubh reaches terminus in the mighty climber's cliff of Stob Coire nan Lochan. Surely those great gullies lead safely down from the knife edge of the Aonach Eagach Ridge? No. Every experienced mountaineer knows that these are false trails that end in severance, hanging above rocky bluffs. To top it all, from the road and the valley floor, the highest summit of them all, the highest in Argyllshire at 1,148m/3,766ft, Bidean nam Bian, is hidden from view.

Landscape and nature is so raw, so elemental, here that at first it is difficult to think beyond it. But there is life here and an abundance of beauty if you are calm and perceptive. Blue rhyolite, white quartzite, ice and snow, tumbling waterfalls, purple heather, crimson-berried rowan, silver-skinned birch, blood-red whortleberry, red stag, golden eagle and invisible ptarmigan – snow white in winter and equally camouflaged in summer.

Man has thrived here and revelled in the power of it all. From the fjord-like sea waters of Loch Leven all the way to the high plain of Rannoch Moor, history and legend litter the landscape. Neolithic cup markings, Bronze Age figurines, Viking graves, the cave of the mighty Ossian and the defences of the blond warriors, the Fionn. And, of course, this is the scene of the most infamous act of treachery in British history – the massacre of the MacDonalds in 1692.

The challenging heights, in the main protected and conserved by the National Trust for Scotland, are the province of the rock climber and mountaineer, while down below scattered farms and the little communities of Glencoe and Ballachulish function through the extremes of the seasons as they have done since the Bronze Age. The magical rowans bear blossom, unfurl their leaves and hang red with berries before the deep savage snows of winter blanket all. Above, beyond the snow-capped

LEFT: Blown by gale and stung by snow, the Scottish flag stands proud below the Glencoe Ski Centre. Legend has it that in 832 AD, an army of Scots faced a Northumbrian army. The Scottish king prayed to St Andrew for help, and saw the saint's sign, a saltire (the heraldic term for a diagonal cross), in the heavens against a clear blue sky. He vowed that if the Scots defeated the English, St Andrew would forever be their patron saint. The Scots won the battle, and from that day the diagonal white cross on a blue background has been the country's national flag.

ABOVE: On the fringe of Rannoch Moor, with Black Mount behind, Blackrock Cottage provides an evocative foreground to the pyramidal Buachaille Etive Mor. A traditional stone-and-timber farmstead lined with pine plank boarding for insulation, the cottage continues to provide snug accommodation for mountaineers. It is now owned by the Ladies' Scottish Climbing Club.

OPPOSITE: At the head of Glencoe and Glen Etive and below Black Mount, the Kingshouse Hotel takes its name from the time when officers responsible for building General Wade's military road were billeted here c. 1750. The inn itself, however, is reputed to be much older, maybe one of the oldest inns in Scotland. To supplement its meagre income it allegedly dealt in contraband, and was undoubtedly frequented by cattle drovers and the clan MacDonald on illicit cattle raids beyond Glencoe. It remains a welcoming inn, popular among mountaineers and climbers, walkers on the West Highland Way and indeed anyone exploring the Highlands of Scotland. It cocmmands, from the comfort of its lounge, a spectacular view of Buachaille Etive Mor.

peaks, the golden eagle rules the air. On the slopes, the red stag stamps his authority across the purple heather.

I have loved this place since my first recollections of childhood. On our annual holiday roaring past Buachaille Etive Mor in motorbike and sidecar – Dad with enormous leather gloves gripping the handlebars, my brother with ridiculously long woollen scarf trailing in the wind, Mum holding my legs – I would poke my head above the canvas canopy wide-eyed with the wonder of it all. Through this photographic essay I hope to share that fascination with you. Let me take you on that journey again, from the wastes of Rannoch Moor to the shores of Loch Leven through the incomparable Glencoe.

The tour

We begin by going over Rannoch Moor with Lochan na h-Achlaise to the left followed by Loch Ba and its rocky islands, clad with silver birch, to the right. After a slight rise, the long fall to the head of Glencoe begins in earnest. The Black Mount group of high hills dominates the scene to the left while wide open space prevails to the right. In winter, red deer, particularly at dawn and daybreak, are a frequent sight.

On the left a road leads to the once isolated Blackrock Cottage, now a mountaineering bothy, and to the Glencoe ski lift up White Corries. Some may consider the latter a rather overbearing presence in such a delicate ecosystem. On the other hand, its visual intrusion is relatively slight, it boosts the local economy, and it does provide some good skiing if you are so inclined. Okay, I'll come clean: my son's first ski experience happened here during work on this book – he loved it! A little further and a road branches off to the solitary Kingshouse Hotel, reputedly one of the oldest inns in Scotland.

A raised arch bridge (with the bridge deck hanging from the arch) leads on over the River Etive with Buachaille Etive Mor, 'great shepherd of Etive', standing proud beyond. This wonderful mountain, with many fine rock and ice climbs,

gaelic place names with their pronunciation and meaning

Name	Pronunciation	Meaning
Achtriochtan	*ak tree-okhin*	field of three streams
Altnafeadh	*ault nam fay*	burn (stream) of the bog
An Torr	*an tor*	rocky hill
An t-Sron	*an trawn*	nose
Aonach Dubh	*oe-nokh doo*	black ridge
Aonach Eagach	*oe-nokh ee-gokh*	notched ridge
Ballachulish	*bala-hoolish*	town of the narrows
Beinn a'Bheithir	*by-an a vay-heer*	great snake mountain
Beinn Fhada	*by-an at-a*	long ridge mountain
Bidean nam Bian	*beed-yan nam by-own*	head of the mountain peaks
Buachaille Etive Beag	*boo-kel etiv beg*	little shepherd of Etive
Buachaille Etive Mor	*boo-kel etiv moar*	great shepherd of Etive
Eilean Munde	*ellin vun-ne*	island of Mundu
Etive	*etiv*	name of a river sprite
Fionn Ghleann	*fyoon glyown*	white glen (valley)
Gearr Aonach	*gear oe-nokh*	short ridge mountain
Glencoe	*glen co*	narrow valley
Inverigan	*inner you-gun*	wooded confluence
Lairig Eilde	*la-rik ay-de*	pass of the hind
Laroch	*laa-rukh*	dwelling site
Loch Leven	*lokh leevin*	loch (lake) of the elm tree
Rannoch	*ranokh*	watery
Sgorr nam Fiannaidh	*skor nam fee-a-nee*	peak of the Fionn, the fair-haired warriors
Stob Coire nan Lochan	*stob kora nan loch-yn*	peak of the corrie of the lochans

stands at the heads of both Glen Etive, running to its left, and Glencoe to its right. Do not turn, but head straight on to pass the buildings of Altnafeadh at the point where the famous path known as the Devil's Staircase leads off to Kinlochleven. Built as a military road under General Wade in about 1750, it linked the forts at Tyndrum and Fort William with the purpose of subduing any further Jacobite aspirations. Today it is followed by the classic long-distance footpath, the West Highland Way.

Round the bend we take the straight to pass Buachaille Etive Mor. A further bend in the road offers a view directly to Buachaille Etive Beag ('little shepherd of Etive') before the road begins to descend into the glen itself. Between parking areas, on a slight bend in the road, the old road (pedestrian access only) bears off to the right. Abandoned in the 1930s when the new road was blasted through the rock, it runs higher than the existing road at this point, offering a dramatic entrance into the heart of the glen. Beyond, before the first rock cutting, a conical masonry cairn can be seen to the right. Recently reconstructed by the National Trust for Scotland, it is thought to be a coffin cairn – a spot where the clans carrying chieftains for burial would stop and rest. A further two similar cairns have been found in Lairig Eilde and Lairig Gartain, the two valleys south and north of Buachaille Etive Beag.

At the second rock cutting, there is a pull-off and limited parking space where a tumbling waterfall thunders down a rock bluff. Here the Allt Lairig Eilde joins the main river down the valley. I have always known this point as the Meeting of the Waters, though properly the Meeting of Three Waters lies downstream. There, the Allt Ruigh, tumbling from the Chancellor north of the glen, having joined the main river, is intersected by the Allt Doire-bheith and the Allt Coire Gabhail flowing from the Lost Valley south of the glen. The ravines form a right-angled cross in the bedrock of the valley floor, and officially create the River Coe.

ABOVE LEFT: This simple arch bridge is a remnant of the old road through the glen. Spanning the Allt Coire Meannarclach, it is built from rocks of andesite lavas and rhyolite, which can be found near the coffin cairn in the upper reaches of the glen. The old road, occupying higher ground, offers unparalleled views down the glen. A simple excursion along its brief length will be well rewarded.

TOP: The cutting for the new road, constructed in the 1930s, reveals attractive pinkish-brown rock with flesh-coloured banding, a typical feature of the region's rhyolite.

ABOVE: A number of dome-shaped cairns around the glen have lately been identified as coffin cairns. Found near meeting places, where important pathways crossed, they are thought to mark the temporary resting points of the coffins of clan chieftains during their final journey. This cairn, recently reconstructed by the National Trust for Scotland, can be found beside the new road at the intersection of Lairig Eilde and Glencoe; others have been found at the heads of Lairig Eilde and Lairig Gartain.

OVERLEAF: Reflections in the still waters of Loch Leven show the buildings of Glencoe and the domed top of the Pap of Glencoe (Sgorr na Ciche in Gaelic, meaning 'breast peak'). This is the view seen by many approaching seafarers – Picts, Scots, Vikings and steamship puffers. It is a relief that we no longer have to face the warlike Fionn warriors once ensconced on the sweeping slopes of the Pap.

RIGHT: A stone-built cottage on the main street near the centre of Glencoe village. High dormer windows raised into the roof are a distinct feature of traditional Scottish architecture. It is likely that the walls of this cottage pre-date the massacre of 1692. The original roof of heather thatch was replaced with Ballachulish slate in the 1700s.

A little way beyond this point a break in the ravine offers a limited parking space on the right. From here, a short path leads up to the top of the rocky knoll, traversed by the old road. Known as the Study, it is located at a strategic point in the valley beneath the Three Sisters, which now dominate the south horizon. Various, mostly ruined, structures may be spotted round about. The view from here is the most rewarding along the whole length of the base of the glen. Look down over the cottage of Alt na Reigh and to the rocky heads of the famous Three Sisters: Beinn Fhada directly above to the left, followed by the formidable rock prow of Gearr Aonach and, last, the great Aonach Dubh, the most influential and expansive of the family.

Beneath the cottage of Alt na Reigh – where once the great climbing pioneer Hamish MacInnes revolutionised snow and ice climbing with his new design of ice axe, the Pterodactyl – a new bridge looks rather incongruous, its red stone parapets a shade too light to rest easily among the darker rocks of Glencoe. The main car parks follow, and offer approach and limited views into the Lost Valley and Coire nan Lochan. Not too long ago, tinkers dressed in kilt and full Highland regalia used to play their bagpipes here to the tourists for a few coins. For me that was part of the Highland experience. Some say that they may have been the true remnants of the clans brutally broken by the subjugation following the 1745 Jacobite rising. Where have they gone?

Achtriochtan farm, currently without a permanent tenant, looks up to the great rift of Ossian's Cave high on the north face of Aonach Dubh. Ossian, a figure of Gaelic mythology, was said to have lived around 300 AD. Next come the waters of Loch Achtriochtan with a view up to An t-Sron and Stob Coire nam Beith's Church Door Buttress. At this point, a minor road bears off right to pass the Clachaig Hotel before leading past the youth hostel to Glencoe village. The Clachaig Hotel is the logical stop-off point for those who have successfully traversed the Aonach Eagach Ridge, and is much frequented by walkers

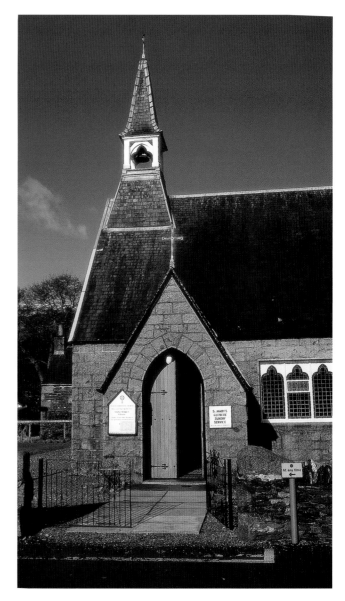

RIGHT: St Mary's, the Scottish Episcopal church in Glencoe, is an elegant steepled building made from striking local silver-grey granite c. 1880. The Episcopal Church was once the stronghold of the Jacobite (Stuart) cause; bonding the clans, it was supported by the Appin Stewarts of Achnacon and Ballachulish, Locheil and his Camerons, and the MacDonalds of Glencoe. They were all closely associated with the three Jacobite failures: the Battle of Killiecrankie, 27 July 1689; the Rising of 1715, and the Rising of 1745–46 under Prince Charles Edward Stuart (Bonnie Prince Charlie). After 1745 the Episcopal Church was reduced to 'a shadow of a shade' but, despite harsh repression and the burning of clan homes, some four hundred faithful were baptised and confirmed during the visit of Bishop Robert Forbes in 1770, saving the Church from extinction in the region.

LEFT: *Prior to the 1970s Ballachulish bypass, the main road used to pass beneath this archway. The steep incline above it once carried the slate bogies from the quarry down to the jetty for shipment. An ingenious gravity-based system employed twin tracks and a large rotating drum, slowed by a great brake. Around the drum ran a continuous steel hawser that connected the full bogies, going down under their own weight, with the empty bogies, which were pulled back up the bank.*

and mountaineers. Nearby, hidden in the woods, can be found Signal Rock, a commanding viewpoint from which the 1692 massacre is said to have been instigated. This area's present claim to fame is as the site of Hagrid's hut in the film of *Harry Potter and the Prisoner of Azkaban*.

The nature of the glen changes markedly at this point. The valley floor widens and the awesome steeps retreat to a safer distance. Conifers occupy the ground around and down from Signal Rock, with a mixture of deciduous trees – birch, ash and rowan – inhabiting much of the riverside space. Two deep valleys, Fionn Ghleann and Gleann Leac na Muidhe, run off to the south to end in heights overlooking Glen Etive. Human habitation becomes more prevalent; below the green slopes of Meall Mor there is a campsite and a National Trust for Scotland Visitor Centre. This is designed in a deliberately low-key fashion, resembling a series of wooden sheds, and replaces a more grandiose centre further up the glen which was removed for environmental and conservation reasons. Although it may look a little lacklustre from the outside, the Vistor Centre is extremely well laid out and informative, with a weather station, a café and an excellent bookshop attached.

The Trust's involvement started when Lord Strathcona put the Glencoe estate up for sale in 1935. There had been growing awareness that the region was of outstanding natural beauty and special importance, and it was felt that it should be protected from commercial exploitation and development to be an area where all had the right to roam free. Between 1935 and 1937 the National Trust for Scotland acquired Signal Rock, a gift from Dr Sutherland, and other land including Aonach Eagach. In all, the Trust purchased 12,800 acres of the glen, thanks to financial help from the Scottish Mountaineeering Trust, alpine and other climbing clubs, the Pilgrim Trust and public subscription.

Opposite the Visitor Centre, another unmistakable landmark feature, the Pap of Glencoe, signals the last of the magnificent heights on the north side before they finally tumble into the salty waters of Loch Leven. Glencoe village follows, and here can be found plentiful accommodation, shops, folk museum, church and the MacDonald memorial monument to the victims of the massacre. North over the River Coe, where it issues into the sea loch, is the hamlet and campsite of Invercoe.

West along the main road is the village of Ballachulish, with its inactive slate quarry now adorned with fact-finding trail and accompanying information boards. Great accommodation, an inn, shops and Visitor Centre make Ballachulish a good base from which to explore the region. Now high and dry above the road, a slate arch beneath an incline once spanned the route taken by our old motorbike and sidecar – what fun! Opposite, floating in the waters of Loch Leven, is the burial Isle of Eilean Munde; above, the magnificent mountain ridges of Beinn a Bheithir. A railway signal standing by the nearby roadside church seems a trifle incongruous – but it's genuine. The 28-mile long branch line from Connel, just outside Oban, to Ballachulish opened in 1903 and was one of the last railways to be built in Britain. Along with many branch lines, it closed in 1966; the road now occupies much of its space.

So on to the Ballachulish bridge, opened in 1975, which replaced the old turntable ferry. It leads to North Ballachulish, an important settlement site of prehistory and the end of our journey. Never mind the dizzy heights of Glencoe, in the old days taking that ferry across the tidal rip of the narrows was adventure enough.

winter

Rain may lash or blizzard blast. There are so many different moods to winter here: the close proximity of the sea and prevailing westerlies battle with a latitude that rivals the frozen tracts of Hudson Bay and snow-clad Moscow. At its finest and coldest, the air can be breathless and all movement stilled under clear blue skies. Rime fingers and translucent curtains of ice hang above pure white snows to mask the blackness beneath. The ptarmigan and mountain hare, masters of disguise, turn pure white, the former with feathery plumage extending to cover its feet and talons. With the rivalries of autumn forgotten, red deer stags socialise along the valley floor. Mountaineers sharpen ice axes and crampons, skiers try on their latest outfits, all hoping for snow.

OPPOSITE: Above the snow-clad flanks of Buachaille Etive Beag a watery moon hangs in the sky, reluctant to move on to the west and give way to the breaking dawn. In Gaelic mythology the thirteen moons of the year all have names and status: this is the height of the period of the Dark Moon, when the full moon begins to wane as January slips into February.

LEFT: A slender rowan splits a boulder beside the road to Glencoe. It was probably propagated from a seed deposited by a bird wiping its beak on the rock after eating rowan berries. Devoid of leaf, berry or flower, it nevertheless presents a powerful image as the magical tree of both Celtic and Viking mythology. Those born under this sign, 21 January to 20 February, use their intuition and higher understanding to enchant and protect; many have an ability to see into the future.

BELOW: Low winter sunshine rakes across the brown heather surrounding Lochan na h-Achlaise on the edge of the watery wastes of Rannoch Moor. The heights behind are those of Black Mount, Clach Leathad (left) and Meall a Bhuiridh (right). This is magnificent country – wild, desolate and untrammelled.

OVERLEAF: Winter sunrise over Rannoch Moor. Once in a while God gets his brush out to paint a sky of awesome beauty – and it really doesn't matter what happens for the rest of the day.

BELOW: A winter's day dawns
down Glencoe. This distinctive
raised arch bridge carries the
main A82 over the young River
Etive before making a long
swoop down the narrows
of Glencoe. Before new
construction in the 1930s,
most of the bridges, canals and
even churches in the Highlands
were designed by the great
civil engineer Thomas Telford
and dated from 1803 to 1823.

ABOVE: Leafless rowan trees stand by the outbuildings of Altnafeadh, with the snow-clad heights of Buachaille Etive Beag framed beyond. This is the last outpost before ascent via the notorious high pass of the Devil's Staircase, which rises to an altitude of some 610m/2,000ft before falling to Kinlochleven.

This is the route followed by the West Highland Way. Around 1750 it was used by General Wade's Military Road and, more recently, c. 1905, by the navvies who built the dam to form Blackwater Reservoir. An obvious stop-off point, it has taken various forms over the years, including inn, whisky den and bunkhouse.

ABOVE: Above the rock cuttings of the road, a flat rock at a bend in the glen provides a breathtaking view. Known locally as the Anvil and more generally as the Study, it is traversed by the old road. Queen Victoria picnicked here, under the guardianship of John Brown, and reportedly remarked, 'What a study!' – so giving it its second name. It is probably the finest location from which to view the power of the Three Sisters on the southern side of the glen. Two of the three are shown here: Gearr Aonach (left) and Aonach Dubh; Bheinn Fhada (not shown) is to the left of the picture.

LEFT: Cascading some 23m/75ft over the hard ignimbrites, this waterfall is called by me the Meeting of the Waters though, strictly speaking, the Meeting of Three Waters – those that officially form the River Coe – is downstream below Alt na Reigh Cottage. These waters are the Allt Lairig Eilde and the Lairig Eilde, tumbling into the river flowing down Glencoe. A lay-by on the south side of the road allows a close view, most impressive after heavy rain or during the spring snow melt.

BELOW: On the south side of the glen, facing north, snow tops the steep dark faces of two of the Three Sisters: Gearr Aonach on the left and Aonach Dubh on the right. Mighty bastions of vertical rhyolite, they provide a heady challenge for rock climbers. The valley between the two, Coire nan Lochan, leads to the high cliff of Stob Coire nan Lochan, whose great gullies often hold snow well into the summer months.

BELOW: A fierce east wind blasts clouds of spindrift – fine ice particles of re-crystallised snow – from the heights of Bidean and Beinn Maol Chalum into the head of Fionn Ghleann. The name means White Glen – apt in these conditions – but it is accepted that the name refers to the legendary Fionn warriors who were fair-haired and blue-eyed. Under conditions such as these the Fionn, or indeed anyone, would be best to stay indoors: the wind chill factor can take the temperature to −50°C and unconsolidated accumulations of snow present extreme avalanche danger.

BELOW: A shaft of sunlight breaks through the storm clouds over Creag Dhubh in the Black Mount hills above the head of Glencoe. The name Creag Dhubh, meaning Black Cliff, was adopted (with the slightly different spelling of Creagh Dhu) by a famous anti-establishment climbing club in the years after the Second World War. The new road of 1931 had opened the area to many more climbers, among them a group of young shipworkers from Clydebank. They formed the Creagh Dhu Club, whose rules were that there were no rules – if you wanted to join, you couldn't. Your face and your beliefs had to fit – if they did you were in, like it or not. The philosophy was one of freedom and common struggle – against the mountain, the elements and the old social order. Talent and effort, boldness and daring, and a love of the great outdoors were the qualities that counted. These men radically changed the face of Scottish mountaineering, putting up a range of rock climbs which are still thought hard today.

BELOW: The dramatic halo of a 'Brocken Spectre' seen high on Sgorr Bhan. This optical phenomenon is experienced only in mountains; its name comes from sightings on the highest peak of Germany's Harz Mountains. You see your own figure, cast as a shadow, in the centre of a halo that consists of all the colours of the rainbow. Here, the dark figure at the centre of the halo is my shadow as I take the photograph; the dark triangle approaching the centre is the shadow cast by the ridge. Far below, bottom right, the white cottages of Ballachulish can be seen through the cloud. Brocken Spectres, once thought to be supernatural appearances, are relatively common on the Scottish mountains. The sun has to lie at a low angle behind you, shining through a clear atmosphere, while below there must be a sea of cloud. Your shadow is cast on to the cloud, around which point the rays of light from the sun are diffracted through the water droplets in the cloud to form the rainbow circle. It is just one of many spectacular natural displays that may be experienced in mountains, and I am always thrilled by them. A note for would-be photographers: turn off auto focus and go on to manual.

BELOW: A fishing boat swings between the burial isle of Eilean Munde and a fish farm below the forested slopes of Coille Charnuis on the north side of Loch Leven. As the wild harvest from the sea begins to diminish and fishing quotas bite the local West Coast fishermen, fish farming is boosting the local economy. Salmon, trout and mussels are harvested on Loch Leven; problems with contamination of the surrounding seas from the farms are still being assessed.

OVERLEAF: At the end of another long day in the mountains the winter sun casts a pink glow on the winter sky above the Pap of Glencoe (right) and the Mamores (left) as the lights are switched on in the blackening Glencoe village far below.

six thousand years of history

The fascinating social history of Glencoe goes way beyond the infamous massacre of 1692. Many have plied their trade here from prehistoric times: Celts, Vikings, and the Lord of The Isles which led to the clan system, modern history and the present day. Despite the relatively recent addition of road and rail, Glencoe has never really been remote – because the sea, the great provider and international highway, leads right to its doorstep.

Prehistory (4000 BC–600 AD)

Discoveries around North Ballachulish have revealed some remarkable evidence. Stone axes and flint arrowheads show Stone Age (Neolithic) activity, c. 4000 BC. On the rock point in Bishop's Bay, on the north side of the Ballachulish Narrows to the east of the bridge, rock art in the form of cup and ring markings can be found. These take the shape of a cup or scallops in the schist rock, the larger two being joined by a deep groove giving some similarity to a dumbbell. Originally thought to be Bronze Age, c. 2000 BC, there is no evidence to disprove that they could be much earlier in origin, perhaps Neolithic. The Bronze Age is also represented by evidence of crannogs – houses built on stilts in shallow lochs. Most exciting in terms of visual impact was a discovery by peat cutters in the Ballachulish moss of a figure carved in alder wood, 1.2m/4ft high, complete with quartz inset eyes, enclosed in wickerwork. Now in the National Museum of Scotland, Edinburgh, the 'Ballachulish Goddess' has been carbon dated to the Iron Age, c. 600 BC.

Within the glen itself are various earthworks and assemblages of boulders and stone walls which are yet to be dated. Ditches and elongated platforms about halfway up the Pap of Glencoe on the direct route from the valley floor are easy to spot. They tie in with the legends of the Fionn warriors supposedly based there and on the peak bearing their name, Sgorr nam Fiannaidh ('Peak of the Fionn'). Bell-shaped or conical

BELOW: Eilean Munde burial isle is the largest of three islands, linked at low tide. Gravestones are still visible on the site of the ruined church (on the left of the picture). Religious activity supposedly commenced here with St Mundu in c. 600 AD. On the nearby island of Eilean Choinneich there reputedly stood a monastery or a series of monks' cells, although no archaeological work has yet been carried out to clarify this.

OPPOSITE: The folk museum in Glencoe village is a stone building traditionally restored with a heather thatch roof, the usual roofing material before slate began to be quarried from Ballachulish in 1693. Open during the summer months, the museum contains a wealth of artefacts found locally that range from prehistoric to modern.

cairns in the depth of the glen and in the offshoot valleys either side of Buachaille Etive Beag are of unconfirmed antiquity.

The burial isles of Eileen Munde, St Mundu's Isle (600–900)

The area was first ruled by Celts, initially Picts and then Scots (who originated from Ireland). Once Christianity arrived, the ancient burial ground was named after St Mundu, who is said to have come from Ireland to join St Columba in his Christian mission. In Irish literature his death is commemorated as occurring in 635 AD. There are three islands, linked at low tide, with a ruined church on the largest. Grave slabs are carved in what is thought to be Celtic relief. The massacred MacDonald chief is buried here; the MacDonalds of Glencoe, the Stewarts of Ballachulish and the Camerons of Onich were all laid to rest here up to 1972, when the last burial took place.

The Vikings (900–1100)

Around the end of the 8th century, the Vikings moved from their established base in the Hebrides to take mainland west coast Scotland. Celtic mythology suggests they were unsuccessful in Glencoe, and that an attack under the Norse King Erragon of Lochlann was repulsed. Perhaps so, but their attacks would have been relentless, and easy sea access into the heart of the Glencoe settlement, a relatively rich farming and fishing community, would most certainly have meant that in time the Vikings held sway. What are thought to be Viking graves in Laroch, south Ballachulish, support the theory of Viking settlement rather than defeat. At the Ballachulish Narrows, east of the bridge on the south side of the loch, a split boulder known as Clach Pharuig is said to mark the spot where the Viking Pharuig drowned when his boat was swamped.

Vikings out, clans in (1100–1500)

Sometime around the 11th century, Glencoe became the property of the MacDougalls, a clan of Viking descent. The Vikings signed away their powers and sailed off in the 13th century. But the MacDougalls then sided with the losing team, and Angus Og acquired Glencoe after aiding Robert the Bruce at the battle of the Pass of Brander. His son, Iain Fraoch, 'John of the Heather', was the forefather of the MacDonalds of Glencoe. The land they controlled along the west coast passed to Clan Donald and in 1354 their leader assumed the title 'Lord of The Isles'. For some two hundred years they ruled as independent kings in western Scotland.

Stormy waters (1500–1700)

Around the beginning of the 1500s, the community of Glencoe was settled and relatively prosperous. Stone houses with thatched roofs of heather and turf provided homes for the people, who grazed cattle, cultivated barley and oats, and fished the plentiful herring. It was not difficult for them to pay the chief and landlord his rent. But all was to change as both England and Scotland moved into a period of social unrest and great turbulence. The lot of the MacDonald clan (also known as the Maclains), was to worsen considerably.

The MacDonalds had become a little too powerful, and were seen as a threat by King James IV. In 1493 he abolished the Lordship of The Isles; from then on it was something of a free-for-all. The MacDonalds, without charter or legal title to their lands, entered the Linn nan Creach, 'age of plunder'. They were determined to hold on to their position le coir a' chlaidheimh, 'by the sword'. And those that live by the sword die by the sword.

There followed some 150 years of cattle rustling and internecine unrest. Wrongdoing on all sides led to acts of revenge, leading to further acts of revenge. With the backing of the government in Edinburgh, the Campbells occupied the richer Lowlands and prospered; the MacDonalds became sidelined as outlandish Highlanders. In 1643 came the Scottish Wars of the Covenant during the English Civil War: the

MacDonalds sided with the Cavaliers and the Campbells with the Scottish equivalent of the Roundheads. Their long rivalry came to a head during the famous Atholl Raid of 1685 and the balance of power shifted once again: the Campbells were now weakened by their stand for Charles II and James VII, and their estates and property became easy prey to the MacDonalds. Huge tracts of Campbell land were pillaged and many Campbell families suffered badly. One family stripped of wealth, pride and fortune was that of Robert Campbell of Glen Lyon. His name will shortly appear again in the black history of this period.

During the subsequent rising of 1689 Alastair Maclain (12th Chief of the Glencoe MacDonalds) took his clan to fight for 'Bonnie Dundee' at the Battle of Killiecrankie. Dundee, John Graham of Claverhouse, was referred to by the clans on the opposite side (including the Campbells) as 'the Bloody Claver'. Dundee was killed and the newly installed Protestant King of England and Scotland, the Dutchman William of Orange, was soon to hold the reins of power. From that moment the fate of Alastair Maclain and his free-spirited, rogueish Clan MacDonald was sealed.

On 27 August 1691, William reluctantly offered to pardon all Highland clans who had fought against him or had raided their neighbours, on condition that they took the oath of allegiance before a proper magistrate by 1 January 1692. Troops were assembled at Inverlochy, Fort William, with the intention of subduing dissenters among the west coast clans. Alastair had four months to make the short journey to Inverlochy and sign. Showing his utmost contempt, he waited until the last day.

Too late. On arrival Alastair was directed to Inverary, near Oban, delayed by government troops *en route* and then kept waiting. Eventually he took the oath five days past the deadline. John Dalrymple, Master of Stair and Secretary of State for Scotland, wrote his fateful orders to the garrison of soldiers at Inverlochy on 11 January: 'You are hereby ordered and authorised to

march our Troops which are now posted at Inverlochy and Inverness, to act against these Highland Rebells . . . to burne their houses, siese or destroy their goods or Cattell, plenishing or cloaths and to cut off the men.' Further to that Sir Thomas Livingstone, Commander-in-Chief of the King's forces in Scotland, wrote on 23 January: 'I understand the Laird of Glencoe coming after the prefixt time was not admitted to take the oath, which is very good news to Us here . . .' In reality, it is questionable whether his being on time would have made any difference; there is no doubt that state, crown and his bitter clan enemies wanted rid of this troublesome and dangerous thorn in their side.

Two companies of some 130 officers and men were despatched on 1 February under the command of Robert Campbell of Glen Lyon. It is said that all were entertained and put up in the homes of the Glencoe MacDonalds for the next ten days. This seems a little strange in the circumstances – odd that 130 soldiers, armed to the teeth and purposely assembled to take care of any dissidence towards the crown, led by a man who had a real and great grievance against you, should be welcomed to your bosom without a murmur. I can't help but feel that Alastair, educated in Paris, a charismatic and a fearless leader, must have had an inkling that something untoward was in the offing.

On 12 February Robert Campbell received written orders to mount a surprise attack on his hosts at five o'clock the following morning, and to kill all MacDonalds under seventy. Major Robert Duncanson, based at Inverlochy, wrote: 'putt all to the sword . . . root out the old fox and his cubs . . .' It is said that a fire was lit on Signal Rock at 5 a.m. on 13 February. The massacre began.

In all, around 38 were killed including Alastair, but remarkably some 300 men, women and children escaped to the hills and, according to legend, into the Lost Valley. Contrary to the orders, the escapees included both Alastair's sons and his

grandson, so the bloodline of the MacDonalds was saved. Terrible though the massacre was, I can't help but think that the 'old fox' played his last hand to some effect. There is no question that he won the propaganda battle. The massacre has long been portrayed as the ultimate betrayal, 'murder under trust', with the ruthless Campbells betraying the benevolent MacDonalds. And to this day the front desk at the Clachaig Hotel bears the sign: 'No hawkers or Campbells'.

John, 13th Chief of the MacDonalds, was allowed the king's pardon and rebuilt the family home at Carnoch. His brother Alastair stood for the Jacobite cause in 1715 and fought alongside John Campbell, son of Robert Campbell who had led the massacre. They lost, and forfeited their estates. Thirty years later, the baby grandson who survived the massacre, another Alastair, now 14th Chief, fought with Bonnie Prince Charlie in the 1745 uprising. Culloden was their last stand, and the Highland Clearances followed with the burning of their houses and the systematic subjugation of the Jacobite clans.

The order changes (1700 to the present)
One year after the massacre, in 1693, slate quarrying began in Ballachulish, showing what the regular working man can achieve with endeavour, ingenuity and community spirit. It is said that Cumbrian quarrymen (perhaps relations of mine?) were imported to lend expertise and get things going. Production peaked around the 1850s when the quarry employed some 2,000 men. So good was the slate here – easily split, durable and highly attractive – that the leading architect Charles Rennie Macintosh used it for The Hill House at Helensburgh in 1902.

Following the 1745 Jacobite rising, General Wade was charged with the task of linking strategically placed forts with military roads along which troops could rapidly mobilise. The road from Tyndrum to Fort William, via Kingshouse and Kinlochleven, was built between 1750 and 1752. This was when Kingshouse was named, when officers and horse were billeted there during the construction of the Devil's Staircase. This section of the road takes a series of zigzags to reach an altitude of 548m/1,800ft before falling to Kinlochleven. It is now the route taken by the West Highland Way, on its traverse from Glasgow and Loch Lomond to Fort William. This road was used for only thirty years, however, before the first road through the glen was constructed in 1785.

Leadership of the MacDonalds continued with the 17th Chief, Ewan, who served as a doctor in India; on his death his estate was inherited by his daughter Ellen Burns MacDonald. It was she who erected the memorial in Glencoe village in upper Carnoch. She subsequently sold the estate to Lord Strathcona of the Hudson Bay Company, Canada. Large tracts of the glen were then acquired by the National Trust for Scotland.

If you cast an eye around the shores of Loch Leven you will see numerous old piers and jetties. Various trade was conducted from here, including the shipping out of slate and the importing of coal and other essential supplies. In the 1900s, with a surge in tourism, a number of steamers also docked here. The Ballachulish ferry, originally a large rowing boat with two balanced planks to carry one car, had graduated to carrying six cars by the time it closed in 1975 when the bridge was opened. It was an exciting trip, racing up with the tide then backtracking to the slipway along the water's edge.

spring

Suddenly the darkness recedes, daylight telescopes into the night. Life, suspended, kickstarts again. Around the MacDonald monument daffodils and lucky white and purple heather burst into bloom. In the woods and sheltered places primrose, celandine, violet, wood sorrel and wood anemones appear as if by magic. Tails of birch and alder catkin bob in the breeze, ash bears a curious fur-like flower while creamy blossom hangs from the rowan. Bluebells and wild hyacinths rampage through field and meadow. Swathes of gorse and then broom go golden. Finally green unfurls. Eagles, peregrines, ravens and buzzards, first with eggs, will soon tend chicks. Fawns run with hinds as the stags, aloof and unfettered, return to the heights. Around Loch Leven and Loch Linnhe, otter are with cub and seal with pup.

OPPOSITE: High in the Lost Valley by the Allt Coire Gabhail a rowan tree bursts into life. The sparkling waters of the allt (stream) are swollen by melt from the snows above. Found between the 'sisters' of Beinn Fhada to the east and Gearr Aonach to the west, hidden from below by huge boulders obscuring the entrance, the Lost Valley has surprising proportions. Once entered, its true magnitude is revealed – the pasture here resembles that of a high alpine meadow. Legend has it that within its confines the MacDonalds secreted stolen cattle and also found refuge after the 1692 massacre.

OVERLEAF: Despite appearances, this is not an active volcano! Rapidly clearing clouds above Glencoe village reveal the Pap of Glencoe to the left and Sgorr nam Fiannaidh to its right. The walk to the summit cone of the Pap reveals breathtaking views and is well worth while should a wet day suddenly dry out. The path ascends through ancient earthworks (ditch and embankment) that correspond with the legendary defences of the Fionn warriors who are said to have inhabited these heights. It is steep, strenuous and longer than it appears – you should allow three hours to go up and return.

OPPOSITE TOP, LEFT: Lady's smock is found in the verge and damp meadows in late April or early May. It is also known as 'cuckoo flower' because it attracts the leaf-hopper larvae which sucks juice from the stem; mixed with air this is the familiar froth known as 'cuckoo spit'.

CENTRE: Lesser celandine, the golden face of spring, flourishes in the many mixed woods and banks of Glencoe.

RIGHT: Sun dappled by the trees shows wood sorrel, growing from a soft moss carpet, at its best. Unusually, the flowers close and leaves droop in stronger sunlight – it is at its best in one-tenth the intensity of normal daylight.

OPPOSITE BELOW, LEFT: The great yellow orb of the marsh marigold, also known as 'kingcup', is a sure sign of spring. It likes soil saturated with groundwater and there's usually plenty of that around!

CENTRE: Wood violet thrives in undisturbed woodland.

RIGHT: Of all the springtime flowers, primroses are perhaps the loveliest. Despite being prolific in the lower reaches and sheltered places of this highland glen, like all delicate springtime wild flowers they should not be picked. We are all responsible for their survival.

BELOW LEFT: It is very difficult to spot the nest of an oyster catcher, another master of disguise in the natural world. In springtime when you stroll along that pebbly beach, take great care not to stand on the eggs. 'Nest' is almost too grandiose a term for this slight basin scraped out of the pebbles, just adequate to retain a clutch of three eggs.

BELOW: Frog spawn at 790m/ 2,600ft on Aonach Dubh a' Ghlinne in late April. Despite large patches of snow still holding the heights, a cacophony of croaking gave away the position of this tiny lochan. It was alive with frogs and thick with spawn – it seemed quite amazing that these small amphibians could survive and prosper at an altitude still in the thrall of winter.

BELOW: A falling spring sun reflecting off the River Coe as it enters Loch Leven below the bridge leading to Invercoe. The main run of salmon and sea trout to the spawning ground high in the River Coe does not pass this way until late August or September, but there will also be a smaller springtime run of these migratory fish.

OPPOSITE: A climber's view from beneath the Rannoch Wall on Buachaille Etive Mor as a great rainbow arcs across the wastes of Rannoch Moor. Hardly discernible in the distance, beneath the flanks of Meall nan Ruadhag, is the remote Black Corries Lodge.

BELOW: In the heart of the glen, gorse sets off Achtriochtan farm which is now owned and managed by the National Trust for Scotland.

OPPOSITE: An impressive cascade near the head of the Lost Valley. The steep path keeps to the right of the fall before climbing on beneath Lost Valley Buttress to Bealach Dearg ('pass of the buttress'). This is a gateway to the high mountain ridge which leads to Argyll's highest mountain, Bidean nam Bian.

OPPOSITE: The view down the Allt Coire Gabhail and the Lost Valley to the deep rift slicing into Sron Gharbh on the north side of Glencoe. Here is the unexpected flat bottom to this secretive valley, which cannot be guessed from the depths of the glen below. Rocks of all sizes, from stream debris to great boulders, dominate the mood. Surely the MacDonalds, returning in springtime to graze their animals, would have constructed some form of shelter in this high pasture, although no visible remains can be seen. Falls of rock, dislodged in the winter's freeze and thaw, may have obliterated all trace.

BELOW: A sycamore below Achtriochtan farm stands with its leaves bursting from bud in late April while the neighbouring ash trees are still devoid of green. The piles of stones and earthworks are the remnants of buildings that stood here before the Clearances.

LEFT: Purple cultivated heather, Erica carnea, flowering January to April, adds early colour to the garden around the MacDonald monument.

BELOW LEFT: White heather, Erica darleyenis, by the MacDonald monument. Travellers, summer walkers, often sold white heather as a good luck charm along with their handmade clothes pegs and besoms.

BELOW: A young larch, the most common of the winter bare conifers, unfurls its bright green needles by the bank of the River Coe. In October these will colour a wonderful golden brown before falling.

BELOW: A common seal pup balances on a rock to warm itself and dry out its fur. Ungainly on land, in the water seals are fast, agile swimmers. Their inquisitive nature means that they often pop up close to boats.

RIGHT: Yellow gorse by Loch Leven.

ABOVE: A view to the summit of
Bidean nam Bian from Stob Coire
nan Lochan. At 1,150m/3,773ft,
Bidean is Argyllshire's highest
mountain. Although the season is
late May, plentiful banks of snow
still hold the heights. Despite
its formidable appearance, in
summer it is a straightforward,
if somewhat strenuous, walk to
the top from the floor of the glen.

ABOVE: Looking directly on to the nose of Gearr Aonach with, at the same height, Aonach Dubh to the right. At a higher altitude to the left stands Stob Coire Sgreamhach at the head of the Lost Valley; to the right is the great cliff of Stob Coire nan Lochan. Trapped in deep dark gullies and hanging corries, snow may linger here beyond spring into the summer months.

OVERLEAF: All is quiet as evening falls. Looking into the bottom of the glen over North Ballachulish, the setting sun casts a pink glow over the west face of Aonach Dubh. The slopes falling from the right are Meall Mor, and from the left Sgorr nam Fiannaidh. The sun-kissed peak in the middle distance is Stob Coire Raineach, which forms the northern top of Buachaille Etive Beag.

geology

Despite appearances to the contrary, rocks don't stand still. Through the science of plate tectonics, we now understand that huge land masses move across the globe over vast periods of time. It is this movement that began the sequence of geological complexities that formed today's Glencoe. Some 500 million years ago the land mass of Laurentia, which included present-day Scotland and America, and the land mass of Avalonia, which included present-day England, were separated by a large ocean. They floated closer together across the earth's crust to join up around 420 million years ago. As these mighty continents crashed into one another, the ocean vanished and the Caledonian Mountains were born out of the same force that created the US Appalachians. Then, around 60 million years ago, the land mass containing America split from that of Britain to float to its current position on the far side of the Atlantic.

The metamorphosed sediments include quartzite, which forms the Pap of Glencoe, schists with lovely folding visible by the road through Onich, and slates exposed in the Ballachulish quarry. The twin peaks of Beinn a Bheithir above Ballachulish Bridge are granite, and many of the peaks surrounding the deep rift of Glencoe are rhyolite, cut through and filled by multitudinous porphyrite dykes of cooled magma. In places these dykes of softer rock have eroded to form water courses, such as the cross-shaped formation in the bottom of the glen below the Lost Valley, known as the Meeting of Three Waters. Most dramatic of all is the great vertical rift of Ossian's Cave on the north face of Aonach Dubh.

Volcanic activity, faulting, folding and jointing complicate the picture further, but the area's most classic feature, first recognised and studied by geologists at Glencoe, is the famous 'ring fault'. A major event in shaping the landscape, this fault line, around five miles in circumference, takes an elliptical journey around the valley, running through the bottom of the glen by the Clachaig road junction and around Bidean to encircle all the peaks south of the valley before crossing above

Buachaille Etive Mor and returning along the Aonach Eagach Ridge. Volcanoes, spewing lava on to the existing beds of metamorphosed rocks, caused a thickening dish-shaped area of rock to become too heavy for the molten granite magma below the earth's crust to support. This basin of rock sank into the underlying cauldron. As it sank, around its edges magma flooded through and under extreme pressure exploded into the atmosphere to refill the bowl with molten rock. These rocks welded together to form beds of hard ignimbrite – the blood-red rhyolite of Buachaille Etive Mor and the dark blue-purple rhyolites of Gearr Aonach and Aonach Dubh.

Despite a complex sequence of faulting and further intrusions of igneous dykes, the 'ring' itself remains as a traceable granite band surrounding and defining the region. You can easily see it for yourself in the old granite quarry by the Clachaig road junction which marks its western extent.

Relatively recently, in geological terms, the scouring effect of glaciation gave us what we see now. During the last major phase, between 25,000 and 14,000 years ago, a huge ice sheet some 1,500m/5,000ft thick covered the area. This flowed and melted to form the interconnecting fjord sea lochs of Loch Leven and Loch Linnhe, which extend round the Island of Mull via the Sound of Mull and the Firth of Lorn before joining the North Atlantic; next stop America. The ice sheet was to return again 12,500 years ago. With the tops of the mountains sticking out above the ice, it flowed down the glen, scouring and polishing and ripping up rocks, deepening the glen and creating the hanging side valleys seen today. A final melt around 10,000 years ago deposited huge boulders and beds of gravel. On Gearr Aonach, the middle head of the Three Sisters, a tottering pile of boulders fell, choking the entrance to Coire Gabhail and creating what we know as the Lost Valley. Years of freezing and thawing produced further shattering of rocks and great fans of scree, particularly evident falling from the Aonach Eagach Ridge.

ABOVE: Along the base of the glen, cutting through the hard ignimbrites that formed the bottom of the caldera, the River Coe and its many tributaries form numerous deep ravines, tumbling waterfalls and crystal clear rock pools. Deposited pebbles of the myriad different rocks show something of the complex geology and subsequent glaciation that formed Glencoe.

OPPOSITE: At Tigh-phuir, Glencoe Bay, a disused stone jetty of Ballachulish slate protrudes into the deep water of Loch Leven. Construction of the support walls, topped by water-shedding cam stones, is remarkably similar to that of the stone walls of the English Lake District. Was this the work of Cumbrian quarrymen, thought to have been brought here for their expertise when quarrying started in 1693? Slate boathouses in various locations along the loch edge in front of Ballachulish are now under a preservation order.

ABOVE LEFT: A white quartz intrusion cuts through the dark Ballachulish slate. Quartz and iron pyrites (iron sulphate, 'fool's gold') are two common minerals found in slate. The iron pyrites form in small cubes, up to 10mm/⅜ in across, which glisten in the sun following a shower of rain; quarrymen call them 'slate diamonds'. The 'rivers' (men who split the slate with hammer and chisel) used to save them in a matchbox for me when I was a lad.

ABOVE RIGHT: The Allt Ruigh stream plunges from Sron Gharbh on the north side of the glen. The striking purple piece is possibly an agglomerate, a mixture of rocks embedded in a finer matrix thought to occur when a volcano blasts fragments far and wide. The larger piece beneath appears to be granite, possibly extruded into the ring fault which formed the edge of the caldera. So much geological history in one little section of stream . . .

flora and fauna

ABOVE: A billy goat and entourage add to the variety of domestic animals within the glen. Goats are traditional in the region and it is recorded that after the massacre many sheep and goats were set loose from the MacDonalds' farmsteads. A herd of goats is now farmed near Glencoe village.

OPPOSITE: Taking advantage of lowland grazing are a red deer hind and last year's fawn. During the depths of winter, the normally shy red deer descend from the heights and can be seen near the road and sometimes outside the Kingshouse Hotel. This is because food is scarce: grazing has been lost under the grip of snow and ice, and what little remains has to be found within the confines of the glen.

In the peat hags and bogs, particularly around the upper reaches of the glen and Rannoch Moor, the ancient bleached white 'bones' of the Old Caledonian Forest can be seen. The most influential factor on the mountain scene is, of course, the purple heather. It grows to an altitude of at least 760m/2,500ft and all three British heathers are represented here. Cross-leaved heath and bell heather flower before ling (common heather), which is most resplendent from mid August. On the extreme heights, alpine lady's mantle and clubmoss are found, and even rare alpine saxifrage. In damp locations, mountain sorrel and meadow rue hang in clusters. Blaeberry and whortleberry (commonly known as 'crowberry') are a feature along the rocky ridges and are often joined by rose-root and the saxifrages – golden, yellow mountain and mossy saxifrage, with spring-flowering purple saxifrage tufting from fissures in the rocks.

For flowers, June and July are the most colourful months, though their scenic influence on the overall mountain picture, the grandeur of the glen, is limited. Many orchids are found around the lower climbs and include heath spotted, fragrant, early purple, marsh, common spotted and small white orchids. Yellow bog asphodel abounds on boggy ground and four-leaved pale yellow tormentil and white heath bedstraw run with the heather. Around the shoreline are thrift (sea pink, which occurs everywhere, even on the heights) and small white scurvy grass.

The wildlife most associated with the Highlands are, of course, red deer and golden eagles. You can see both around the Glencoe region, and there is much more. In the air are peregrines, buzzards, ravens, kestrels and sparrowhawks. By the shore is a host of birdlife including oyster catchers and herons, and many different ducks, sawbills, waders and divers. Mammals other than deer are well represented, though most prove very elusive indeed: they include wild cats, pine-martens, red squirrels, mountain hares, otters, badgers and feral goats.

OPPOSITE TOP, LEFT: The vivid colour of the evergreen cypress contrasts with the white winter snows outside the entrance to the Kingshouse Hotel. Photographs indicate that this delightfully decorative tree may have been planted in the 1970s.

RIGHT: Ling follows bell and cross-leaved heather: it is the most resplendent of the heathers in August and September.

OPPOSITE BELOW, LEFT: A green hairstreak butterfly on yellow gorse in late April. The male hairstreak is very territorial and displays itself on one bush awaiting a female – just like the bar at the Clachaig Hotel on a Saturday night! However, once disturbed it is hard to follow because it makes rapid jerky flights among the scrub.

RIGHT: A rowan blossom starting just after the fresh leaves have unfurled.

LEFT: Hooded crows in flight. Native to Scotland and rarely seen south of the border, the 'hoody' has a distinctive grey body and is easily recognisable in the Highlands.

BELOW LEFT: A nest in a rowan tree with four hooded crow eggs. Before the new leaves break, the nests are easy to spot, looking like untidy clusters of sticks in the forks of the branches. On the inside they are much neater and are lined with moss, wool, hair and sometimes feathers. The carrion crow and hooded crow are distinctly different-looking birds but their eggs, usually laid in May, are indistinguishable.

BELOW: A master of disguise, the ptarmigan – seen here among white quartzite rocks on Sgorr Bhan in early September – is mottled white and grey in autumn to blend with the rocks and heather. In winter it will turn completely white, including plumage grown over its legs and talons to preserve heat. Even in extreme conditions it is rarely seen below 610m/2,000ft.

BELOW: Out on the hills the hardy Scottish blackface sheep are with lamb in late April and early May. Any earlier could spell disaster if there were a sudden cold snap, snowfall or heavy rain. Less tough breeds born at this time of year are initially kept indoors. Blackface ewes make excellent mothers and will defend their offspring against any perceived threat, as you may find out should you walk too close.

OPPOSITE: At home high in the mountains blackface sheep forage for food. Despite the harsh conditions they yield a good lamb crop and wool clip. Their wool is very fine and goes into many of the best Axminster and Wilton carpets. The breed spread during the nineteenth century from the Border areas to the Highlands and Islands, and also to Northern Ireland and the United States.

LEFT: Red deer stags congregate in considerable numbers during the winter. They are distinguished from the hinds by their branched antlers, which they shed each February and re-grow between April and July, gaining more branches the older they get. In the rutting season during October mature stags compete for the hinds, challenging opponents by bellowing and defiant posturing. Clashes of antlers can occur, and stags sometimes sustain serious injury.

BELOW: Deer fawn are born in June, and can be left safely by their mothers for long periods in patches of heather. Man is now the only real predator to threaten the red deer.

BELOW: Highland cattle, with Aonach Dubh and Glencoe behind. This unmistakable breed is one of Britain's oldest, most distinctive and best known – with a long, thick, flowing coat of rich hair and majestic sweeping horns. It has remained largely unchanged over the centuries – this is the very same breed that was reared, traded and probably rustled by the MacDonalds. Its survival is testimony to its remarkable quality and character.

RIGHT: Highland cattle thrive and breed where no other could exist – on areas of poor mountain land with high annual rainfall and bitter winds. They are remarkable for their longevity: many highland cows continue to breed beyond eighteen years of age, having borne fifteen calves. Just before I took this photograph, the majority of the herd were frolicking and stampeding around the field just for fun. They are protective mothers, so I resisted the urge to get closer – something to do with the size of their horns, I think.

summer

Tourists briefly stop and spill out on to the levelled stone car parks mid glen. They point to the entrance of the Lost Valley, raise their eyes to Stob Coire nan Lochan, shudder and quickly head for the craft shop and café. Once we used to camp wild around the glen drinking in the intoxication of it all, the sweet honey fragrance of the purple heather, the crimson sunsets, the open night sky bright with shooting stars, the roaring silence of the mountains all around. We watched families of eagles spiral effortlessly into the outer stratosphere on their journey to infinity. It never rained and there were no midges on those halcyon highland summer days – well, not so that it mattered!

OPPOSITE: A view north over the long ridge of Beinn Fhada from Stob Coire Sgreamhach. Down to the left, deep in cloud shadow, lies the Lost Valley. Clear skies and high cloud reveal the vastness of the mountainscape around Glencoe.

BELOW: Best viewed from the old road near the Clachaig Hotel, the west face of Aonach Dubh is a favourite haunt of the climber. Its deep gullies and vertical buttresses are the home of many challenging rock and ice climbs.

OPPOSITE: High above Glencoe is 'Big Top': one of the great rock climbs on the west face of Aonach Dubh, first climbed by legendary Scottish climber Robin Smith in 1961. I made my first ascent around ten years later. Incredible exposure and lack of protection made it a memorable experience. Today, with modern equipment, it is classed as one of the easier 'extreme' climbs hereabouts. The prominent figure on the skyline is belaying while, above, the lead climber weaves his way through the difficulties.

OVERLEAF: The rocky summit of Stob Coire Sgreamhach, complete with cairn, stands at the head of the Lost Valley and east of Bidean nam Bian. The steep descent from its rocky heights to the ridge of Beinn Fhada involves negotiating the 'Bad Step': walkers should beware. Shortly after taking this photograph, probably distracted by the thought of the impending difficulties, I left a pair of binoculars on the cairn. Did anyone find them?

BELOW: Moss campion is very much a hardy plant of the Scottish Highlands. I photographed this one on Beinn a' Bheithir's summit of Sgorr Dhearg at an altitude of 1,006m/3,300ft. Elsewhere it has been recorded at a height of around 1,310m/4,300ft. It usually flowers between June and July.

RIGHT: A cairn built from the white quartzite outcropping on Sgorr Bhan above Ballachulish. It is a useful way marker along the shoulder for walkers.

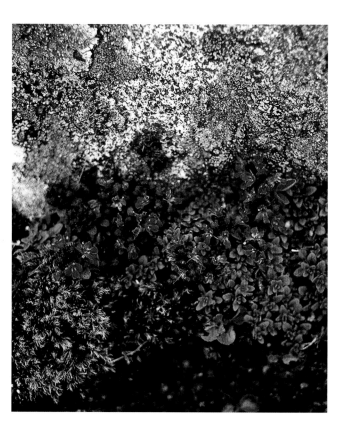

OPPOSITE: Above the Lost Valley, Chris Thorpe tackles the extremely difficult east face of Aonach Dubh by a route named Freakout. A hairline crackline and a few flake holds on the vertical rhyolite wall allow upward progress for the strong and bold. A long way below can be seen the road through the glen and, hardly discernible, the main roadside car parks.

BELOW: Dwarfed by the grandeur of the mountains, a party of walkers moves along the ridge between Stob Coire Sgreamhach and Bidean nam Bian.

BELOW: Through the notch in the Aonach Eagach Ridge between Stob Coire Leith to the left and the Pinnacles to the right, a view over the Mamores reveals the distinctive rock nose of Ben Nevis's north-east buttress.

LEFT: The central portion of the Aonach Eagach Ridge, seen from beneath the east face of Aonach Dubh above the main road and Achtriochtan farm, high in the Lost Valley. Running the length of the northern boundary of the glen, this knife-edged crest offers one of the most exciting mountain outings in mainland Britain. Between Am Bodach to the east and Stob Coire Leith to the west there is no safe descent: once undertaken, a traverse must be completed or a return made along the ridge. The full traverse is a formidable undertaking, offering sensationally exposed scrambling to round the Pinnacles.

BELOW: Clear and pollution-free, the sky in the Highlands sometimes provides reward enough. This short, straight bar of spectral colour is an interesting optical phenomenon seen above the glen – a circumzenithal arc. It arises from refraction through ice crystals that include a 90° angle: the light enters a horizontal face and leaves through a vertical one.

OPPOSITE: Seen from near Signal Rock, the deep rift of Clachaig Gully shoots up the flanks of Sgorr nan Fiannaidh. Purple ling heather adorns the foreground. A classic ascent of the gully was first made in May 1938 by Bill Murray and party. Today, the usual descent from the Aonach Eagach Ridge leads down the left edge – the route is plainly visible here. However, in places it skirts precariously close to the vertical walls of the gully; because of erosion of the path, anyone following this way should exercise great caution.

BELOW: The mists swirl on Beinn a Bheithir over the waters of Loch Leven, seen from the campsite at Invercoe.

OPPOSITE: Buachaille Etive Mor, a pyramid of blood-red light rhyolite, is one of the most evocative mountains in the Highlands – and its many craggy facets, which rise some 458m/ 1,500ft from the moor, provide a wonderful climbing ground. The deep shadow on the right is Great Gully and the central shadow marks the famous Crowberry Gully. Left of this lies the superb vertical Rannoch Wall, defined by Curved Ridge.

BELOW: Down in the bottom of the glen, below the Lost Valley, the dark green, tree-lined cross in the volcanic bedrock marks the Meeting of Three Waters, seen here from high on Gearr Aonach. Beyond this confluence, with the various waters confined to steep-sided rocky ravines, the river officially becomes the River Coe.

OPPOSITE: On the edge of the car park by the roadside in the centre of the glen, with the spectacular backdrop of the high Stob Coire nan Lochan and the dark nose of Aonach Dubh, a lone piper plays in the next coachload of tourists. Officialdom now seems to have stamped out the activities of these travellers. While some may feel this has detracted somewhat from the charisma of the area, others may prefer the silence of the mountains.

legend, myths and magic

With such a stunning melodramatic landscape as Glencoe you would expect tales of legend. Celtic mythology relates that this was the home of Fingal (known also as Fionn MacCumhail), a giant and leader of the Feinn warriors. The Feinn or Fionn (meaning 'white') were supposedly a race of blond, blue-eyed warriors who lived around Sgorr nam Fiannaidh (the peak that forms the western terminus of the Aonach Dubh Ridge) and the Pap of Glencoe.

It is told that the Norse King Erragon of Sora warred against the Feinn, sailing his ships to the mouth of the Coe and alighting at Gleannan Fhiudhaich, a flat field where he erected tents. These fields became known as Laroch (the Laroch Inn is well worth a visit). The Feinn dug four large ditches on the flanks of the Pap for defence and living quarters until they could gather the whole tribe together. The hillside became thickly wooded and they couldn't be seen, and hence they thwarted their aggressors. Earthworks in the form of ditches, and stone and earth walls, show that indeed somebody at some time operated on this fabled battleground.

Another version has it that Fingal and the Fionn defeated the Vikings in battle. King Erragon sailed up Loch Leven with forty ships. Most of the Fingal menfolk were away hunting, and Fingal kept the aggressors talking until their return. Erragon then suggested that each side should slug it out with 140 of their best warriors on the field of Achnacon. The Scots won, but the whole thing was repeated six times until the Vikings finally retreated. At West Laroch, south Ballachulish, eleven grave slabs, now known as the Ringed Garden, are thought to be of Viking origin.

The spectacular Ossian's Cave high on the north face of Aonach Dubh is said to be the home of Ossian the poet, son of Fingal, thought to have lived around 300 AD. He must have been a good climber, too, to get up there in the first place. In the 1760s a Scottish poet, James Macpherson, published a reworking in English of these Gaelic stories, purporting to be 'A fragment of Anciant Poetry collected in the Highlands of Scotland translated from the Gaelic or Erse language'. *The Works of Ossian* caused a sensation in Europe, and the book was translated into over 25 languages. He followed it by *Fingal* in 1762. After decades of controversy, these poems are now mostly thought to be the work of Macpherson's imagination.

The Glencoe hHighlander, as with country folk everywhere, has many tales of witches and magic. Bean Nighe was a naughty: see her washing her clothes in the River Coe and you are doomed. Of course, she appeared the night before the massacre. Corrage was another nasty figure: for some incomprehensible reason she was to be given a Christain burial on Eilean Munde, but the sea went wild and she had to be buried at Tigh-phuir, where the main road now goes. Something to ponder on a wild dark night as you walk home from the pub!

OPPOSITE: High above Achtriochtan farm on the formidable north face of Aonach Dubh is the deep vertical rift of Ossian's Cave. Legend has it that Ossian, poet son of Fingal, dwelt here. Geology says it was formed by erosion of a softer vertical dyke of rock. It isn't difficult for competent climbers to reach its floor, but once there you will find it disappointingly sloping and inhospitable. The early pioneer climbers placed a log book in a tin box there for those who made the ascent to record their visit; Dougal Haston, angry young man of the 60s, reputedly threw it out. This was some time before he rose to international stardom with his first ascent of the south face of Annapurna with Don Whillans. Haston was killed in the Alps in an attempt to out-ski an avalanche.

autumn

Subtly the colours are changing to brown and gold. The light seems gentler, more even. On the tops when those distant white showers arrive, sweeping over Loch Linnhe and Loch Leven, they fill the air with myriad jewels of ice. As in time immemorial, salmon and sea trout fill the lower rocky pools of the River Coe, waiting for the waters to swell and bear them to the high spawning grounds. Poignantly, the bellowing roar of the red deer stags can be heard in the high corries and across the wastes of Rannoch Moor: the rutting season has begun.

OPPOSITE: Looking down to Alt na Reigh Cottage from the Study. This view, enjoyed from the old road through Glencoe, is regarded as one of the finest in the Highlands.

BELOW: With a sprinkling of early snow on the west face of Aonach Dubh, the sun breaks through the clouds to illuminate Signal Rock (centre) in golden light. If the conifers on the left look vaguely familiar to Harry Potter fans it is because this was the site of Hagrid's hut in the film Harry Potter and the Prisoner of Azkaban (the hut was removed after filming).

OPPOSITE: Around a waterfall in Clachaig Gully, crimson rowan berries, ash, silver birch, fern and heather all begin to change to their autumnal colours

BELOW LEFT: The blood-red berries of whortleberry reach maturity in autumn. They are seen here among lichen on the heights of Aonach Eagach.

BELOW RIGHT: Autumnal hawkbit.

BELOW LEFT: The debris of autumn.

BELOW RIGHT: The crimson berries of the rowan (Sorbus aucuparia) brighten the day.

OVERLEAF: A rainbow beyond the quartzite summit cairn of Sgorr nam Fiannaidh. The bow is cutting through the narrow straits of Loch Leven at Caolas nan Con (bottom) and Ben Nevis (top).

ABOVE: The Three Sisters of
Glencoe seen together from the
old road. Left to right they are
Beinn Fhada, Gearr Aonach and
Aonach Dubh. In the foreground
the route of the old road can
be seen winding round into
the body of the glen. Offering a
spectacular entrance, it is a route
well worth walking for those who
have a few spare moments. The
high snow-clad alpine-looking
peak is Stob Coire nan Lochan.

ABOVE: Looking down from the Study with the cairn by the old road. This is reputedly the scene of Queen Victoria's picnic with John Brown, where they encountered the over-indulgent attention of the press (some things never change). Nearby are various memorials – one a climbing hut with the words: 'Jim Memories Die Hard 3rd March 1973'.

BELOW: From Sgorr nam Fiannaidh looking west over Loch Leven, Ballachulish Bridge, Loch Linnhe to Garbh Bheinn, and the distant hills of Ardgour.

OPPOSITE: Above the banks of the River Coupall, the white cottage in the foreground, Lagangarbh, now serves as a climbing hut and is owned by the Scottish Mountaineering Club. It provides an excellent point of access to the climbs on Buachaille Etive Mor which stands beyond.

BELOW: Water tumbling from the Lairig Eilde forms this dramatic roadside waterfall.

BELOW: Snow comes to the
heights of Stob Coire nam Beith
above Achnambeithach House
and Loch Achtriochtan. Below
this point the road splits, with
a minor road off to the right first
passing the Clachaig Hotel
before entering the head of
Glencoe village.

ABOVE: A fine view up the length
of the glen looking eastwards
to the Kingshouse Hotel and
Rannoch Moor. The rocky steeps
are those of Aonach Eagach to
the left and the two Buachailles
to the right.

ABOVE: Over Achnacon with the sun slanting down Fionn Ghleann to illuminate the erosion-scarred flanks. Beyond this point the glen closes and the impressive steeps rise to Aonach Dubh to the south and Aonach Eagach to the north.

OVERLEAF: As the last light leaves the glen and evening falls, framed by the shoulder of An t-Sron, spectacular skies are reflected in Loch Achtriochtan.

climbing and mountaineering

For those who love mountain adventure, walking, climbing and winter mountaineering, Glencoe is superb. In terms of impressive crags, vertical steeps and historically significant ascents it is undoubtedly one of Britain's premier locations. Additionally the high crags of Stob Coire nan Lochan and Bidean nam Bian hold good snow and ice conditions for long periods during the winter months. Crag access, too, is relatively short and straightforward and this is another major factor in the popularity of the glen. Of course, with some 2,300mm/90in plus of rain per year, there is no guarantee of good weather and occasionally the biting midge does make life unbearable. But nothing is perfect!

There are a number of very good and interesting low-level walks, but the high peaks and ridges are mainly the province of the real mountaineer. The competent hill walker may aspire to top Buchaille Etive Mor, Bidean nam Bian and make a summer traverse of the Aonach Eagach Ridge, but in anything less than perfect conditions these become demanding outings and fall into the category of mountaineering. Days out on these hills are serious affairs. Distances are substantial, route-finding can be difficult and the weather fickle. Suitable preparation and equipment are essential.

Although it should only ever be called upon as a last resort – it really is up to individuals to do all they can to extricate themselves from the mountains – a very efficient Mountain Rescue team now operates out of Glencoe village. Professional in expertise and highly sophisticated, it is still run by volunteers. In 2001 they rescued 23 individuals but, tragically, had four fatalities.

Let me take you on a quick trip through the best areas – the sublime steeps of Glencoe. From the 1890s, Buachaille Etive, with its central gullies and many different rock faces, and the beautiful Rannoch Wall were at the forefront of climbing development. In the late 1950s and 1960s, the huge and imposing Slime Wall came to prominence, and today the awesome overhanging wall Creag a'Bhancair provides the challenge. The nose of Gearr Aonach and the rock walls of the Lost Valley also have much to offer. On the heights, the great cliff of Stob Coire nan Lochan supplies both fine rock climbing and the most reliable winter mountaineering conditions in the region. Aonach Dubh, stretching from its East Wall right across the Ossian's Cave area and on to the West Buttress, is a major area to rival even that of Buachaille. Finally, above the end of Loch Achtriochtan and the house of Achnambeithac, below the summit of Bidean nam Bian, the Church Door and Diamond Buttress form two magnificent climbing grounds.

The history of climbing here is a fascinating tale of daring, skill and ingenuity. It began with primitive equipment and an overwhelming passion to scale the heights by the most aesthetic and challenging routes possible with, as they say, 'friction, faith and nothing else at all'. To put things in context and add perspective, I'll run through some of the key players.

The first recorded ascent, to one of the most obvious and intriguing features in the glen, was made in 1868 when Neil Marquis climbed to Ossian's Cave – he was purported to be a local Gaelic-speaking shepherd who lived at Achtriochtan farm down below the cave. The next route, the start of climbing as we now know it, was by Norman Collie who did Collie's Climb on Buachaille in 1894. Collie was a charismatic figure who did much to pioneer climbing in Britain, the Alps, the Canadian Rockies and even the Himalayas. He was also a scientist who made claims to isolating rare gases, producing the first neon light and taking the first X-ray photographs.

Harold Raeburn, a founder figure of the Scottish Mountaineering Club, made the first ascent, in summer, in 1898 of the great Crowberry Gully splitting the Rannoch face of Buachaille. In the first year of the new century, the two photographic brothers George and Ashley Abraham, who were based in Keswick in the Lake District, climbed the Direct Route up Crowberry Ridge. In the 1920s J. H. B. Bell put up the difficult North Face Route, again on Buachaille.

OPPOSITE: A thousand feet above the glen, two climbers tackle the vertical sweep of Rannoch Wall. Their route, known as January Jigsaw, was first climbed in 1940: it is one of a number of great climbs on this most spectacular cliff.

LEFT: Buachaille Etive Mor, gateway to Glencoe and the Highlands, home of some of the finest climbs in the whole of Scotland. Below the towering bastions of snow-dusted rock can be seen the black climbing hut of Jacksonville, long time home of the Creagh Dhu.

In the 1930s Percy Unna, President of the Scottish Mountaineering Club, had the vision to see the potential conflict between commercial development and conservation, and was determined to protect Glencoe and the Scottish mountains. Of Dutch and German extraction, he had climbed extensively in the Alps and had a particular affinity with the unique wildness and unspoilt nature of the Scottish hills. Unna embraced the aims of the Trust and set about marshalling those around him to good effect. Through his efforts, the Trust aquired further parts of the glen including Bidean nam Bian and Buachaille Etive Mor. As well as leading the appeal for money and influencing others, Unna was the largest, although anonymous, individual contributor. Importantly, he and other mountaineers laid down a set of rules, now known as the Unna Principles. These included that the Trust should 'undertake that the land be maintained in its primitive condition for all time with unrestricted access to the public'. The Trust adapts and honours these principles in a rapidly changing world where hill use is considerably greater than in Unna's day. Today, with minimum environmental impact in mind, it has built a new Vistor Centre at Inverigan. It has converted Achnacon Steading into the Leishman Mountain Rescue Laboratory, which also serves as a base for the Trust's Ranger Service. Recent purchases include An Torr woodland and the Inverigan campsite.

Bill Murray was at his most productive in Glencoe prior to the Second World War, making the first winter ascent of Shelf Route on Crowberry Gully in 1937 and the first ascent of Deep Cut Chimney on Stob Coire nam Beith in 1939. He also climbed in the Alps and the Himalayas. Murray will always be remembered for his writing, and in particular his wonderfully evocative treatise on the development of Scottish climbing, *Mountaineering In Scotland*. Captured during the war, he spent its latter years in an Italian prisoner of war camp. Without recourse to diary or written record, it was here that he carefully wrote the book on scraps of paper. It was published in 1947 – a fantastic feat of memory and one of the classic works of mountain literature.

After the war the old order began to change, with the working-class lads of the Glasgow shipyards forming the Creagh Dhu club. The hut they built still stands by the banks of the River Coupall, shadowed by the cliffs of Buachaille. They dominated the hard climbing scene for thirty years and included John Cunningham, whose Gallows Route in 1947 brought in a new era of difficulty; with the great Don Whillans, he worked out the line of Carnivore in the 1960s, opening up Creag a'Bhancair for future generations of hard men. Patsy Walsh, wearing bottle-bottom glasses, climbed cutting-edge routes all over Britain.

Hamish MacInnes, a civil engineer, turned his ingenuity to making the first all-metal ice axe, the revolutionary Pterodactyl. The name says it all – it was a hook-shaped short ice axe that completely changed the way climbers tackled vertical ice. With this tool 'Big' Ian Nicholson, one-time landlord of the Kingshouse Hotel and leading climber, climbed the two hardest ice

RIGHT: A walker begins his ascent of the last pinnacle on the magnificent Aonach Eagach Ridge.

FAR RIGHT: Starting out on the first long pitch of Big Top, first climbed in 1961, on E Buttress of the west face of Aonach Dubh. Beyond the overhang lies a vertical rib with scant protection and 122m/400ft of difficult and demanding climbing. Fancy your chances?

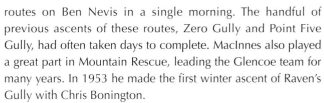

routes on Ben Nevis in a single morning. The handful of previous ascents of these routes, Zero Gully and Point Five Gully, had often taken days to complete. MacInnes also played a great part in Mountain Rescue, leading the Glencoe team for many years. In 1953 he made the first winter ascent of Raven's Gully with Chris Bonington.

In the late 50s and early 60s Robin Smith climbed some of the finest, boldest and most difficult routes, both summer and winter, in Britain. Even though equipment and safeguards have since improved beyond recognition, his first ascents still demand considerable respect. His legendary routes, Shibboleith, Yo Yo and Big Top, climb audacious sweeps of rock in different parts of the Glen and constitute some of the most magnificent extreme climbing to be had. Among his companions, brilliant and influential climbers in their own right, were Jimmy Marshal and Dougal Haston. Looking back at his legacy of routes it is hard to believe that Smith died, climbing in the Pamirs, at the age of just twenty-one.

In the 70s Murray Hamilton with Grogblossom (Slime Wall) and Dave Cuthbertson with Bannockburn (E Buttress, Aonach Dubh) brought Scottish standards up to those being achieved on the intense scene south of the border. Quietly spoken and slightly built, Cuthbertson ('Cubby'), a professional mountain guide, went on to pioneer a host of difficult routes in both summer and winter; he is undoubtedly one of Britain's most influential and accomplished all-round climbers. His routes are landmark ascents in the long and rich history of Glencoe

climbing: Elliot's Downfall in 1979, a vertical free-standing pillar of ice which sometimes hangs from the face of Aonach Dubh; the Duel in 2000, awesome mixed winter climbing on Stob Coire nan Lochan; and the Railway Children in summer 1986, so called because the brick-red overhanging face of Creag a'Bhancair was thought to resemble the inside face of a railway tunnel. The latter, along with Graeme Livingstone's Fated Path, sported bolt protection and was another step forward and a break with tradition in the history of Scottish climbing.

Influential raids by Sassenachs include cheeky schoolmaster Ed Grindley's the Clearances on Aonach Dubh in 1976, and ever-so-cool-headed Pete Whillance's the Risk Business on Creag a'Bhancair. Now the crags wait for the next generation. For sure, there is a wealth of rock and ice for those with vision and the ability to turn dream into reality.

index